ON THE ROAD

BARRON'S

Books in the
WATCH OUT! Series:

WATCH OUT! Around Town
WATCH OUT! At Home
WATCH OUT! Near Water
WATCH OUT! On the Road

First Edition for the United States and Canada published in 2006
by Barron's Educational Series, Inc.

Text copyright © Claire Llewellyn 2006
Illustrations copyright © Mike Gordon 2006

Published by Hodder Children's Books in 2006

All inquiries should be addressed to:
Barron's Educational Series, Inc.
250 Wireless Boulevard
Hauppauge, New York 11788
www.barronseduc.com

International Standard Book No. 13: 978-0-7641-3324-4
International Standard Book No. 10: 0-7641-3324-1

Library of Congress Catalog Card No. 2005926320

Printed in China
9 8 7 6 5 4 3 2 1

WATCH OUT!
ON THE ROAD

Written by Claire Llewellyn

Illustrated by Mike Gordon

BARRON'S

We all use roads from time to time.

When we're out on our bikes ...

catching a bus ...

or driving in
the car.

There are all kinds of vehicles on the roads—trucks, taxis, police cars, and vans.

All this traffic makes the roads very busy.

Cars, trucks, and vans are powerful machines. They are fast and very heavy.

Look what happens when they hit something.

What could happen if they hit you?

Roads are very dangerous places. When you're walking along them, it's important to be careful.

Stay on the sidewalk, next to an adult.
What could happen if you ran ahead?

Sometimes we have to cross the road. This can be tricky and needs a lot of care.

Luckily, there are places that make it safer.

Always choose the safest place to cross the road. One good place is at a traffic light.

You push the button to change the lights. How do you know when it is safe to go?

A crosswalk is another good place to cross a street. Crosswalks don't have buttons or lights.

You wait on the sidewalk until the traffic stops.

This may take a moment or two. Cars need time to slow down and stop.

How do you know when it is safe to go?

17

Sometimes you need to cross the road and there are no special crossings.

This is a nuisance if you want to cross quickly to see a friend or to buy an ice cream.

But NEVER run out into
the road. What could happen if you do?

19

Always cross the road safely. First, find a place where you can see the road clearly.

I can't see. Let's go down a bit.

Then, stop by the curb and look both ways. Listen for traffic, too.

When the road is empty, walk straight across, and look and listen as you go.

When you walk along roads at night, you need to take special care.

Drivers cannot see you well in the dark.

How can you make yourself stand out? How can you make yourself safe?

Can you keep yourself safe when you're in a car? Everyone has to wear a seat belt –

the driver ...

the passengers ...

and baby, too.

A seat belt helps to keep you safe.

What would happen if you
didn't wear one?

Have you ever played on the sidewalk?

Playing outside is a lot of fun, but what could happen if you slipped off the curb, or chased a ball into the road?

Roads are not the best places to play.
Can you think of somewhere safer?

Roads are busy, dangerous places.
But we can all learn to use
them safely.

Keep looking ...

keep listening ...

keep safe!

Notes for parents and teachers

Watch Out!

There are four titles currently in the *Watch Out!* series: *On the Road, Near Water, At Home,* and *Around Town.* These books will prompt young readers to think about safety concerns both inside and outside the home, while traveling in a car, and even while on a trip or enjoying the outdoors. The lessons illustrated in all four books will help children identify important safety issues and potentially dangerous situations that they may come across in their everyday lives. Gaining the ability to recognize potential dangers—as well as being instructed on how to avoid these hazards—will allow readers to be more aware of the world around them. Whether at home, at a park, by the pool, or on a road trip, this series offers helpful tips and information on a number of common, everyday scenarios children should *watch out* for.

Issues raised in the book

Watch Out! On the Road is intended to be an enjoyable book that discusses the importance of road safety. Throughout, children are given the opportunity to think independently about what might happen if they do not pay attention to road safety issues. It allows them time to explore these issues and discuss them with their family, class, and school. It encourages them to think about safety first and how they can make themselves safe.

The book looks at vehicles that go on the road—cars, trucks, vans, etc. It asks questions about what happens when cars hit something, especially what happens if a person is hit by a vehicle.

It is also full of situations that children and adults will have encountered. It allows a child to ask and answer questions on a one-to-one basis with you. How can you make yourself stand out? How can you make yourself safe? The illustrations help with ideas and suggestions.

Being safe on the road is important for everyone. Can your children think of an incident in which they have crossed a road between two cars, or been unable to find a safe place to cross? How did this make them feel? The book tackles these and many other issues. It uses open-ended questions to encourage children to think for themselves about the consequences of their behavior.

Suggestions for follow-up activities

Try doing a traffic survey to see how many cars, trucks, etc. go along the road. Make a picture collection of different types of vehicles and display them in a book or on a wall.

Investigate which materials make good reflectors by using a flashlight in a dark box.

Act out scenes of people trying to cross busy roads, either on a driveway or on the playground. Children could take different roles as cars, vans, pedestrians, etc.

Invite a road safety officer into school and interview him or her about road safety issues. Alternatively, contact your local road safety officer to come to school and talk to the children.

http://www.nysgtsc.state.ny.us/kid-tran.htm
New York State Governor's Traffic Safety Committee's Traffic Safety Kid's Page offers a variety of activities, facts, and links about street safety.

Books to read

Blakley, Cindy, et al. *The Look Out Book: A Child's Guide to Street Safety.* Scholastic, 1987.

Chlad, Dorothy. *When I Cross the Street (Safety Town).* Children's Press, 1982.
Street-crossing rules for both urban and rural areas.

Hartmann, Jennifer D. *Kristofur Kitty: Crossing the Street.* Dorrance, 2003.
Kristofur Kitty teaches children how to safely cross the street.